HIDDEN TREASURES

NORTHERN KENT VOL II

Edited by Steve Twelvetree

First published in Great Britain in 2002 by
YOUNG WRITERS
Remus House,
Coltsfoot Drive,
Peterborough, PE2 9JX
Telephone (01733) 890066

HB ISBN 0 75433 972 6
SB ISBN 0 75433 973 4

FOREWORD

This year, the Young Writers' Hidden Treasures competition proudly presents a showcase of the best poetic talent from over 72,000 up-and-coming writers nationwide.

Young Writers was established in 1991 and we are still successful, even in today's technologically-led world, in promoting and encouraging the reading and writing of poetry.

The thought, effort, imagination and hard work put into each poem impressed us all, and once again, the task of selecting poems was a difficult one, but nevertheless, an enjoyable experience.

We hope you are as pleased as we are with the final selection and that you and your family continue to be entertained with *Hidden Treasures Northern Kent Vol II* for many years to come.

CONTENTS

Barrow Grove Junior School

Christopher Eldridge	1
Billy Cooper	1
Katie Dodsworth	2
Jamie Pledger	2
Warren Richards	3
Georgette King	3
Holly Last	4
Chloe Birch	4
Jade Girt	5
Lewis Sidders	5
Fae Thomas	6
Lewis Bond	6
Abigail Thrower	6
Tanzim Miah	7
Diva Jefferies	7
Matthew Ball	8
Harry Parkhill	8
Emma-Louisa Vallis	8
Nathan Rixson	9
Jake Simms	9
Honour Mahlangu	10
Jake Lock	10
Jennifer Bidgood	10
Robert Cherrison	11
Ryan Stevens	11
Emily Byrne	12
Jamie Warren	12
Joanna Calver	12
Jade Wilson	13
Emma Kemp	13
Luke Grant	14
Azaria Cubitt	14
Stevee Butt	14
Mia Stevens	15

Gabriella Lake	15
Jasmine Akhurst	16
David Drury	16
Amy Foreman	17
Martyn Baverstock	17
Alise Carstens	18
Cameron Richmond	18
Danielle Thomson	19
Samantha Inge	19
Lauren Crannis	20
Kasey Oldman	20
Jamie Cripps	21
Emile Carstens	21
Avril Jarrett	22

Bobbing Village School

Jade Baker	23
James Stowe	23
Nicola Myers	24
Kieran Rogers	24
Gareth Collins	25
Emma Lacy	26
Jordan Hardeman	27
Samantha Bance-Foster	28
Zacharrie Smith	28
Lee Wood	29

Featherby Junior School

Joanne Stickells	29
Chantelle Matthias	30
Alistair Salmon	30
Emily Scullard	31
Keeley Butler	31
Laura Ewing	32

Grove Park CP School

Gemma Short	33
Katy Fosbraey	33

Lauren Thrift	34
Kellie Jacques	34
Hilary James	35
Melanie Hope	35
Kane Makepeace	36
Christopher Shortall	36
Sophie Ulyatt	37
Hannah Cheeseman	38
Jack Wetherell	38
Emma-Rose Ellis	39
Poppy Davis	39
Robyn Cesary	40
Stephanie Kenyon	40
Charley Servis	41
Sammy Singleton	42
Lee Burke	43
Liam Kenyon	44
David Baker	44
Amy Hanley	45
Laura Underdown	45
Rachel Foulger	46
Mia Harbour	46
Rachelle Grubb	47
Sennen Thrift	47
Jasmine Ives	48
Tazreen Beasley	49
Rachel Foreman	49
Alastair Rushworth	50

St William Of Perth RC Primary School, Rochester
Sophie Rowlinson-Rogers	50

Senacre Wood Primary School
Gemma Kitchenham	51
Jordan Clarke	52
Tye Williams	52
Felicity Bax	53
Bethanie Jones	54

Sophie Boatman	54
Kirsty Milner	55
Shaun Whiffen	56
Lucy Stratton	56
Amy Boatman	57
Jayleigh Nicholson	58
Gemma Smith	58
Daniel Tucker	59
Emma Russell	59
Terry Simmons	60
Jack Maxwell	60
Emma Winter	61
Jessica Barber	61
Kerry Mason	62
Lia Josling	63

Shernold School

Eleanor Webb	63
Kirsty Keep	64
Lydia Jakob-Grant	64
Elora Williams	64
Jade Waymouth	65
Rebecca Reardon	65
Lexy Payne	66
Grace Stanford	66
Victoria Webb	67
Harriett Cowen	67
Ellie-Bliss Chirnside	68
Jenny Cosgrove	68
Rebecca Harris	69
Harriet Massie	69
Christina Mo	70
Abigail Pile	70
Isabelle Loader	71
Bethany Gerrish	71
Abby Savage	72
Bethany Sidwell	72
Alexandra Browne	73

Eleanor Oliver	73
Jessica Rogers	74
Cara Heffernan	74
Michaela Savage	75
Grace Rudgard	75
Lauren Smith	76
George Edwardes	76
Megan Rumball	77
Shelby-Jo Bellamy	77
Jessica Moss	78
Nancy Watts	78
William Lay	79
Lesley Connor	79
Lourdes Webb	80
Olivia Moss	80

Sherwin Knight School

Clare Stally	81
Charlotte O'Brien	81
Annie Edwards	82
Daniel Gardner	82
Karissa Bristow	83
Daniel Andrews	83
Jake Chapman	83
Lucy Buckle	84
Holly MacDonald-Heaney	84
Tessa Marshall	84
Jade Buckley	85
Luke Fauklin	85
Charlotte Ashdown	85
Samantha Louise Francis	86
Tuncay Albay & Jordan Wright	86
Charlie Tullett	86
Alex Stanley	87
Sherry Kay	87
Racheal Noble	87
Laura Howse	88
Liza Smith	88

Natalie Georgiou	89
Lucy Naish	89
Kyle Collins	90
Kelly Pike	90
Becky Anne Bell	91
Megan Emily Bowne	91
Bethany Riddle	91
Kiera Mae Butler	92
Ashley Mark Stanley	92
Alexander Stephen Lane	92
Lewis Herring	93
Matthew Pamflett & Kierran Boden	93
Alex Potter	94
Sarah Chohan	94
Leah Deaves	95
Kirsty Lou Mayle	95
Victoria Watson	96
Michael Wright	96
Shannon Groom	97
Kierran Boden, Ben Conroy & Tuncay Albay	97
Grace Lidsey, Danniella Butcher & Robyn Morris	98
Daniel Harris	98
Rebecca Harold	99
Hannah Conybear	99
Oliver Sparling	100
Hannah Jane Springate	100
Victoria Betts	101
Luke Wickenden	101
Cherene Ellis	102
Sarah Clayton	102
Dylan Tweedy	103
Bianca Freeman	103
Samantha Wilkinson	104
Ben Conroy, Terry Milton & Zach Annand	104
Lauren Wiles	105

Carrera Still   105
Charlee Green & Charlotte Hall   106

Woodlands Primary School
        Gemma Thompson   106
        Bobby Williams   107
        Sam Cantlon   107
        Shelley Dawson   108
        Laura Vann   108
        Laura Vassiliou   108
        Tanita Bullen   109
        Christopher Roberts   109
        Stefan Koutsouris   110
        Leigh Turner   110
        Charlotte Rowe   111
        Bijan Fard   111
        Stacey Scott   112
        Benjamin Pugh   112
        Stuart Anthony Urquhart   113
        Lisa Inkin   113
        Laura Holmes   114
        April Paterson   114
        Kyrsty Rookes   115
        Keely Rookes   115

The Poems

COLOURS

As white as a snowflake hanging from a young tree.

As pink as a pig playing in the mucky mud.

As green as grass as it sways in the gentle breeze.

As red as a devil in a fiery cave.

As yellow as a daffodil lying in the sun.

As black as tar across the hard ground.

As orange as a mango hanging from an old tree.

As gold as sand sliding into the blue water.

Christopher Eldridge (9)
Barrow Grove Junior School

COLOURS

As yellow as the morning sun sparkling in the twilight.

As pink as a pig's tail in the dirty mud.

As green as the spiky grass moving with the breeze.

As black as a sticky, slimy insect.

As white as the glistening snow, it sparkling on the hard, icy, cold floor.

As orange as a round, juicy mango.

As blue as a bird singing in the soft breeze of the day.

Billy Cooper (9)
Barrow Grove Junior School

COLOURS

As blue as the ocean, swirling across the smooth and gentle sand.

As red as strawberries, fresh and hanging on spiky prickles.

As golden as the lovely sun, sparkling, glowing high up in the
clear blue sky.

As green as the leaves, hanging from the huge brown trees, rustling in
the gentle breeze.

As yellow as a daffodil, swaying around in the wind.

As black as the night sky, shadows in the moonlight.

As pink as the rosy pig, rolling around in the dirty brown mud.

As brown as a little puppy, playing with his chewed up toys.

Katie Dodsworth (9)
Barrow Grove Junior School

COLOURS

As yellow as the sun glittering all over the shiny sky.

As green as an apple glowing on the tree as silently as a tiny mouse.

As blue as the ocean soaking along the coasts.

As black as the tar coming from the grubby, noisy machine.

As gold as the sand with coloured shells on the warm, sandy beach.

As pink as the sweet smelling rose sitting silently in the ground.

Jamie Pledger (9)
Barrow Grove Junior School

Colours

As yellow as the blazing sun in the pale sky.

As red as a rose swaying side to side in the breeze.

As blue as a butterfly's wings flying steadily through the golden sky.

As white as a daisy's petal flying about in the afternoon breeze.

As green as grass swaying side to side in the gentle breeze in
spring's early days.

As black as a spider strolling across the wooden floor, then scuttling
into his hole.

As silver as stars twinkling in the night sky.

As gold as the glistening sand blowing in the night breeze.

Warren Richards (8)
Barrow Grove Junior School

My Magic Box

My box is made from a horn of a unicorn living in the cold, bitter forest.

The hinges are made from the sparkle of an oyster's tooth.

It is lined with a golden thread from an angel's wing that is dangling
in the sky.

Inside my box I keep the sunrise in its magical dressing gown.

I hide my box under a loose floorboard that holds the sounds of an
earthquake's tremble.

Georgette King (9)
Barrow Grove Junior School

Colours

As blue as the shining sky that glitters and sparkles in the bright sky.

As yellow as the bright sun that twinkles in the deep blue sky.

As green as a juicy apple that tastes so good to eat.

As red as hot lava that makes everything glow.

As white as frozen snow that makes you really chilly.

As pink as a beautiful rose that stands proud in a cheerful garden.

As silver as the delightful bar that gleams across the lion's cage.

As gold as the twinkling sand that glows beyond the sea.

Holly Last (8)
Barrow Grove Junior School

Colours

As pink as your lovely soft and smooth skin.

As red as a beautiful rose swaying in the gentle breeze.

As blue as the lovely clear sky looking down on me.

As white as the freezing snow falling very slowly, melting as it touches
my nose.

As green as the refreshing grass sitting in the golden sun.

As yellow as a lovely daffodil swaying in the gentle breeze.

As orange as a juicy, round mango.

Chloe Birch (8)
Barrow Grove Junior School

MY MAGIC BOX

My box is made from the hardened scales of a fighting dragon,
falling from Heaven's ladder.

The hinges are made of a rainbow's smile, sitting in the shining palm of
the sun's hand.

It is lined with the single raindrop of a lonely cloud that glistens in the
corner of my eye.

Inside my box I keep the pumping heart of a star,
sitting on top of the moon's glint.

I hide my box inside an empty-hearted rainbow
that cries a golden teardrop.

Jade Girt (9)
Barrow Grove Junior School

MY MAGIC BOX

My box is made of a shooting star's cry and the rumble
of a volcano's heart.

The hinges are made from a purple rose petal as it gently
drifts to the floor.

It is lined with a shimmering star's smile, glistening in the still,
dark night.

Inside my box I keep the golden-coated beak of a raven.

I hide my box in the moon's smile hanging by a thread
from an angel's wing.

Lewis Sidders (9)
Barrow Grove Junior School

SUMMER

The lemonade people are drinking is fizzy, ice-cold and bubbly
The beaches are full of people sunbathing in the sun
The children are playing in the blue, blue sea
Children are making sandcastles and playing in the sand
People are baking in the sun as ice creams are melting
Birds are singing, people are paddling in the water
People fishing in the lake on a hot summer's day
As the summer sun sparkles in the sky
Everyone is off school
They are all going on their holidays.

Fae Thomas (8)
Barrow Grove Junior School

ANIMALS

A   nn has a cat,
N   orman has a hog,
I   have a bat,
M   um has a dog,
A   dam has a bear that flops,
L   uke has a frog that hops,
S   teven lives in a zoo!

Lewis Bond (8)
Barrow Grove Junior School

DAYS OF THE WEEK

Monday's the day that jumps high,
Tuesday's the day that eats pie,
Wednesday's the day that does swing,
Thursday's the day that makes rings,

Friday's the day that does leap,
Saturday's the day that does heaps,
Sunday's the day I like best because I'm going back to school
Tomorrow!

Abigail Thrower (10)
Barrow Grove Junior School

MY FAVOURITE COUNTRY - BANGLADESH

B lazing hot, sunny day in Bangladesh
A dventurous villages to be explored,
N ice, friendly people in Bangladesh
G rowing crops all over the village so there will be some
L ovely, steamed rice to eat
A ride on a boat would be a lovely treat
D own the meandering river
E veryone is welcome to explore the country
S ee the beautiful, natural world
H owever, the most annoying things are mosquitoes.

Tanzim Miah (9)
Barrow Grove Junior School

ANIMALS

A nimals crawl and some are very small
N asty snakes sliver into the wet grass
I nsects are sometimes small
M onkeys climb into trees and pick off leaves
A nimals are very small and tall
L ittle insects are very small and skinny
S ome animals are quite tall and cool.

Diva Jefferies (8)
Barrow Grove Junior School

My Magic Box

My box is made of a crystal's glow.

The hinges are made from wisdom's rage.

It is lined with a ring from Saturn's flame.

Inside my box I keep the morning's glory from the sun
as it rises at dawn.

I hide my box inside the cry of a heart's smile.

Matthew Ball (9)
Barrow Grove Junior School

My Magic Box

My box is made of a cloud's bright heart, beating on the tip of an
iceberg.

The hinges are made from the sun's burning veins.

It is lined with a computer's hard-earned smile.

Inside my box I keep a tarantula's wing flying in the current of the sea.

I hide my box inside the tick of a clock.

Harry Parkhill (8)
Barrow Grove Junior School

Who Could Be Out There?

Do I have to go hunting tonight?
The bears and wolves will give me a fright
I'd rather stay here in the warm
So I don't get battered and torn
But who could be out there?

I don't like the way they scream out
When they see me skulking about,
I'd rather stay here,
Where there's nothing to fear
But, who could be out there?

Emma-Louisa Vallis (10)
Barrow Grove Junior School

MY MAGIC BOX

My box is made of the magic from a starless night.

The hinges are made from the sound of a tiptoe on a whisper
of the wind.

It is lined with the cracking noise of a heart breaking.

In my box I keep honey dust floating on a moon's beam.

I hide my box in a star, sparkling from the heavens' galaxy.

Nathan Rixson (9)
Barrow Grove Junior School

MY MAGIC BOX

My box is made of an angel riding on a unicorn's heart
around the world.

The hinges are made from a snowdrop dripping from a rainbow's star.

It is lined with the broken heart of an exploding volcano.

Inside my box I keep the moon dancing on the sun's heart.

I hide my box in the crack of an egg as it shatters into the misty air.

Jake Simms (8)
Barrow Grove Junior School

COLOURS

As white as snow falling from the clouds that drift across the
dimly lit sky.

As green as the beautiful grass in summer that blows in the
southern wind.

As pink as a piglet playing happily outside in the sun's warm rays.

As orange as the afternoon sun that warms every corner of the
Earth's crust.

Honour Mahlangu (9)
Barrow Grove Junior School

COLOURS

As yellow as the sun sparkling dreamily in the deep blue sky.

As green as an apple growing in a valley's garden.

As red as a fire burning hot in the kitchen's hearth.

As black as the night sky standing proudly in Heaven's expanse.

Jake Lock (8)
Barrow Grove Junior School

MY FAMILY

My dad is Paul
He thinks he's cool.

My mum is Donna
She's our family honour.

My big sister's Clare
She's got ginger hair.

My other sister's Rachael
She's getting a facial.

My name is Jennifer,
I ride my bike quite far.

Our cat's name is Gizmo
She likes to bite our big toe.

Jennifer Bidgood (10)
Barrow Grove Junior School

COLOURS

As blue as the ocean twinkling in the morning sun.

As red as blood as it drips onto a crystal floor.

As black as the night skyline that glistens in the distance.

As gold as the bright sun that blazes in the midday rays.

As white as crisp snow falling from the lifeless sky.

As pink as a pig playing in the summer's meadow on a hot, sunny day.

Robert Cherrison (9)
Barrow Grove Junior School

INSECTS

I nsects are sometimes small
N o insects are bigger than a person
S tick insects are long and skinny
E longated, slimy worms slide under the ground
C reepy spiders hide in the garden
T ricky flies are hard to catch
S tingy bees make honey in the beehive.

Ryan Stevens (8)
Barrow Grove Junior School

MY MAGIC BOX

My box is made of the last sparkle that has drifted from a star's tip.

The hinges are made from a square sun travelling around Saturn's rings.

It is lined with the soothing voice of an elephant glittering in the sky.

Inside my box I keep a dragon's golden teardrop.

I hide my box in the sun's smile.

Emily Byrne (9)
Barrow Grove Junior School

MY MAGIC BOX

My box is made from the hard glint of a frozen hailstone.

The hinges are made from the silky skin of a petal's yellow cheek.

It is lined with the cheeky smile of a pencil's tip.

Inside my box I keep the world's shining eyelash.

I hide my box in the sparkly blink of a teddy's smiling eye.

Jamie Warren (9)
Barrow Grove Junior School

CALM

Shouting and screaming
It's giving me a headache
Need to be calm
Quiet as a lake.

All this noise
Need to get away
I hate it
This is a bad day.

Joanna Calver (9)
Barrow Grove Junior School

MY MAGIC BOX

My magic box is made of the breath of a rainbow's voice.

The hinges are made from the pumping heart of a rain cloud.

It is lined with the silver smile of a sparkling snowflake.

Inside my box I keep the sun's perfect smile.

I hide my box at the end of the north-east wind.

Jade Wilson (8)
Barrow Grove Junior School

MY MAGIC BOX

My box is made of the dew from a snowdrop's frost.

The hinges are made from the sparkle of a waterfall's drop.

It is lined with the tear from a sunset's whisper.

Inside my box I keep a puppy's dream floating in the life of Heaven.

I hide my box in the point of a rainbow's curve,
stirring in a glittering dream.

Emma Kemp (9)
Barrow Grove Junior School

COLOURS

As blue as the sea spreading over the sandy beach.

As red as a rose swaying side to side in a garden's bed.

As green as grass stirring in a light breeze.

As yellow as the sun rising in the morning's rays.

As pink as a pig rolling around in a cool barn on a hot summer's day.

Luke Grant (8)
Barrow Grove Junior School

THE FIRE AND THE WATER

Fire can burn,
Fire is bright,
Fire is most powerful light.

Water is cool,
Water is calm,
Water glistens in my palm.

Azaria Cubitt (11)
Barrow Grove Junior School

THE DUSTBIN FIGHT

The dustbin fights
With all his might
Rubbish thrown in
Then back out
Shouting that smells
'Don't want that about!'

Stevee Butt (10)
Barrow Grove Junior School

IF I COULD FLY...

I rose up to the dusty clouds
Higher,
Higher,
And higher.
I felt amazed and very happy for myself to fly
Lower,
Lower,
And lower.
I could see the bird's eye view,
Getting even lower,
Lower,
And lower.
I flew over the waves of the sea,
Across,
Across
And across.
I could see the land,
The land,
The land,
The land.

Mia Stevens (10)
Barrow Grove Junior School

WHITE AND BLACK

Creamy milky, frosty, white snow,
Stripy zebra we don't know.
Fluffy clouds in the sky
Seagulls and seals are singing away.
The walls are being painted again
White is the colour I like most.

Gabriella Lake (9)
Barrow Grove Junior School

THE SPRING AND SUMMER, AUTUMN AND WINTER

When it's spring it's quite hot,
The bulbs shoot up.
Blossom comes from the trees,
All pink, white and different colours.
Summer, it's really hot and sweaty,
The sun really shines.
Orange and yellow, gold and red,
I can't believe my eyes.
In autumn time
The sun goes down a bit
The leaves change colour
Red, brown and yellow
They crunch as I step on them.
When it's winter
It's really cold
Everything's white with snow,
I play on my sleigh and have snowball fights
And then it's time to go.

Jasmine Akhurst (7)
Barrow Grove Junior School

MY BEST FRIEND

My friend is cool,
My friend's eyes are blue,
He is the best person in the world
My friend Ryan Underwood.

David Drury (8)
Barrow Grove Junior School

COLOURS

As blue as the shining sky twinkling across the ocean's bed.

As yellow as silky bananas growing in the bending trees.

As white as shimmering snow flickering in the night's flame.

As pink as pig's skin as it sleeps in the quiet of the barn.

As black as tar slipping off a lamp post that is sweltering
in the midday sun.

As gold as the glistening sand in the afternoon breeze.

As brown as the tree's trunk that is swishing in the air.

Amy Foreman (8)
Barrow Grove Junior School

MY MAGIC BOX

My box is made of the silver scent from a star's glow,
standing silently on a volcano's breath.

The hinges are made from the golden heart of a dragon's voice.

It is lined with the soul of an unborn baby, flying to the sun's warmth.

Inside my box I keep the speech of a camel escaping from the moon's
glare.

I hide my box in the golden heart of a fluffy cloud that is happily
playing with the sun's rays.

Martyn Baverstock (9)
Barrow Grove Junior School

MY LABORATORY

In my laboratory everything goes crazy,
Like changing grass into a daisy.
Having fun making solutions
And thinking of ways to stop pollution.
Things bubble and explode making a loud noise,
I take apart and put together toys.
Electricity with static waves,
And studying bats in dark, dark caves.
Chemical reactions with acids and alkali,
Figuring out why wasps can fly.
I can find out why planets orbit the sun,
So come to my laboratory and we'll have so much fun.

Alise Carstens (11)
Barrow Grove Junior School

COLOURS

As blue as the twinkling sky on a summer's day.

As red as the Devil's hostile eyes in Hell's dungeons.

As gold as the glistening sand that sits on an endless beach.

As white as the fluffy clouds that happily appear at dawn.

As green as the juicy apple that hangs on a swaying tree.

As silver as the shining metal that reflects the light from the
early evening's sun.

Cameron Richmond (8)
Barrow Grove Junior School

RABBITS

Jumping, jumping all around
I never stay long on the ground
I'll be gone for just a while
But I'll be back to make you smile.

I will sleep where I oughta
And I'll have carrots and water.
If I could have a loving mate
Who I would love and never hate.

Could I have a cosy place?
Where I'll have a happy face
Could I have a little comb?
Before I settle in my home.

Danielle Thomson (11)
Barrow Grove Junior School

MY MAGIC BOX

My box is made from the sparkle of a shooting star and sweat from the
sun's brow.

The hinges are made from the heart of a down-pouring cloud that can
hear the voice of the Earth's crust.

It is lined with a mermaid's foot dancing in the middle of eternity.

Inside my box I keep the sound of the calm sea that is trapped inside a
Portuguese seashell.

I hide my box inside the cry of a cloud sailing on the Arctic wind.

Samantha Inge (9)
Barrow Grove Junior School

THE CD DANCE

Crash, bang, wallop
As she jumped right off the side
She started dancing round and round
And then went to a glide.
She jumped and sang and pranced around
I felt like going to the ground.
She wasn't playing the song I wanted
All she was doing
Was what she wanted.
I was getting so annoyed
She was having so much fun
I pulled the plug on her so quickly
She didn't know just what had hit her
She was such a bad CD player!

Lauren Crannis (11)
Barrow Grove Junior School

MY MAGIC BOX

My box is made from the tip of a snake's tail dancing with
the sun's ray.

The hinges are made from a star's glow dangling from the tip of Mars.

It is lined with a giant's teardrop mixed with star juice.

Inside my box I keep a fairy's wing flying to the heart of eternity.

I hide my box in a crystal ball filled with the light from a moonbeam.

Kasey Oldman (9)
Barrow Grove Junior School

MY MAGIC BOX

My box is made of the powers from a shooting star.

The hinges are made from the glint of a moonbeam cornered in
Mercury's beating heart.

It is lined with the sparkling glamour of a slug's trail.

Inside my box I keep the drip of a roaring flame escaping from
a dragon's fire.

I hide my box in the voice of a tomato pip,
squashed on an ocean's wave.

Jamie Cripps (9)
Barrow Grove Junior School

MY BEST FRIEND

My best friend isn't a fairy
But is very hairy.
My best friend has a sense of smell,
But can't ring the doorbell.
My best friend can catch a bird,
And he's on his third.
I've got mice, rats, cats,
Even pigs.
But
My best friend is my dog.

Emile Carstens (9)
Barrow Grove Junior School

THE DREAMS OF THE HAUNTED HOUSE

The lights
Have blown,
The fire
Has faded,
I'm scared,
Stiff.
My bones
Are shaking
My friend
Has vanished.
I am on
My own.
I turn
Around,
Monsters have
Come.
My luck
Has changed
I open
My eyes
It is
Morning now.
I have
Survived.

Avril Jarrett (10)
Barrow Grove Junior School

IN THE FOG

In the fog
There stands a dog
He stands by a log
While a man does jog.

In the fog
There stands a dog
He is as wet as can be
He shakes as he soaks me.

Now in the fog
There stands a man and a dog
They are as wet as can be
They must feel colder than me!

Jade Baker (10)
Bobbing Village School

CHRISTMAS

Christmas is here,
Just for me.

Easter is here,
Just like Christmas.

Valentine is here,
Just for love and chocolates.

My birthday is here
Just for presents and money.

James Stowe (11)
Bobbing Village School

TIME

Time is precious to me
It does not sting me like a bee.
It flies so quick
Just like a second of a click
As you can see it flies so fast
I wish I could go into the past.
It is a shame you can't change time
Sometimes times can be fine.
Where does it go?
When you want it to go faster it always goes slow.
Tick tock
The sound of a clock
A second, a minute, an hour,
The time has great power.

Nicola Myers (9)
Bobbing Village School

MY PLAYSTATION

My PlayStation is the best
I play it all day
My mum gave me a test
I passed it.

I always buy some more,
Game, game, game!
Three hours is my law,
I break it every day.

I always play with my friends,
Sometimes one game explodes
After one day
It got sold.

Come back Mr PlayStation
We need you all day,
Jay likes to play twenty-four hours
Come back we need to play.

Kieran Rogers (11)
Bobbing Village School

MY BEST FRIEND

This is my best friend
He is all of these:
He has a wart on his nose
And growing freckles on his toes,
He's tall and fat and also a fool,
Plus he thinks he's very cool,
My best friend is a practising wizard
But all he can do is make snowy blizzards.
His eyes are the colour of green wibbly wobbly jelly
And his bum is as big as a widescreen telly.
His knees are knocked and his eyes are crossed
Plus sometimes all he can say is
Squassshhh!

Gareth Collins (9)
Bobbing Village School

THE HOUSE

You go through the door and step inside
I am going to take you for a little ride
Through the lounge with the painted walls
Mind the carpet, everyone falls.

Back through the hallway, past the stairs
Into the kitchen where everyone stares
The pots and pans are piled up high
Underneath is where the cutlery lie

The stairs are in front of you
Go up, go up,
And good luck
To the bathroom.

The bathroom has a blue touch to it,
And the radiator is a perfect fit,
Look at the bath, nice and clean
Look at the sink with a sheen.

Come out now, you are in the bedroom,
Look around, we have the loft soon,
Next comes the loft, a very yellow colour
And the other rooms are very duller.

Now you have seen the house,
Can I tell you a secret?
It's not my house, it's my doll's house.

Emma Lacy (10)
Bobbing Village School

Oops

How many times have I been told
I really am getting too old
To keep forgetting
And then regretting
The mistakes I make
My parents just can't take
I'd really better escape before
They put their foot down
And show me the door.

Although it's quite unfair
I know
I've been threatened more than once to go
I can't believe it though I must
I really need to gain their trust.

I really thought I had it all
When I came running out of school
My hat, my coat, my bag, my ball,
I must have looked the biggest fool
When halfway down the road I yelled,
'Mum - I'm gonna be expelled!'

How many times have I been told
I really am getting too old to keep forgetting
And then regretting
My homework.

Jordan Hardeman (10)
Bobbing Village School

I'M NOT LOOKING FORWARD

The leaves are brown
The sky is grey
I'm not looking forward to school today.

The teachers are mad,
The children are bad,
So I'm not looking forward to school today.

It's raining again,
The wind is strong,
The day sometimes drags and seems so long.

So I'm not looking forward to school today
I'd rather go outside and play.

Samantha Bance-Foster (9)
Bobbing Village School

LIFE

Life is a breeze,
So we are led to believe.
Life can be good,
Especially how it should.
Life can be bad,
As it is always sad.
And life can get rough,
When the going gets tough.
That's the end of my life tale
Come back again when the ship sets sail.

Zacharrie Smith (9)
Bobbing Village School

SNAKES

Snakes are slithery,
Snakes are slimy,
Snakes make sounds,
The sounds are like ssssss.

Some people don't like snakes,
They will be sorry.

So snakes are slimy,
Snakes are slithery,
Because they come from a place called Slitheren.

Lee Wood (11)
Bobbing Village School

DOLPHIN, DOLPHIN

Dolphin, dolphin you look so sad
Why are you always treated so bad?
Here you are alone in the tank
The rich man is the one you can thank.

Are you dreaming about being free
About jumping up high and whistling with glee?
I wish I could save you and send you back home
To be with your family and not here alone.

If I could make that wish come true
Would you take me away with you?
Dolphin, dolphin, I feel so sad
Leaving you here to be treated so bad.

Joanne Stickells (10)
Featherby Junior School

TWIN TOWERS

Two towers so tall make me feel so small
Excitement filled my body
As I stretched my neck
I froze with fear when I saw the plane
It's going to hit
It's going to hit.
The engine roared
I heard screams and cries
As clouds fell from the skies.
People running everywhere
Here and there
All of a sudden silence filled the air
Water dripped from the tower so small
There was no noise at all.
I stood there in disbelief
I ask who and why.

Chantelle Matthias (10)
Featherby Junior School

HIDDEN TREASURE

They're everywhere
You find them in your garden
Or in the sea.
They could be gold or silver
Or in your house.
They could be in the coral reef
Or in a heap
On the shore.
Hidden treasures are everywhere.

Alistair Salmon (11)
Featherby Junior School

TREASURE

Treasure, treasure where are you?
We have to find you
Before the others do.
Your shining gold,
Your glistening box
Oh! Where are you?
In the sand
Or in the rocks
Or in the sea.
Oh! Where?
Oh! Where?

Emily Scullard (9)
Featherby Junior School

HIDDEN TREASURE

Hidden treasure is my pleasure
Underground to be found.
There are golden coins
And necklaces that glisten.
Rubies and emeralds shine with gleam
Which set the jewels to beam.
After that it's time to go home
To find outside the doorstep a little gnome.
When it's night they're all asleep
No one can make a little peep.

Keeley Butler (8)
Featherby Junior School

PRAYER FROM POVERTY

Help me defeat my awful life
Support me through my tough and arduous times
Encourage me when my hopes scurry off
As ahead my future shines.

Make me notice my promising chances
My life of sorrow and of pain I abhor
When I dream of freedom my heart dances
Help me to heal my soul so sore.

Life on the streets is not a piece of cake
Days of grief, trouble or no feelings at all
By the end of the daytime my feet sting and ache
Occasionally I wish I were a bird that could fly over any wall.

Remind me when my road is bumpy
That life can be changed by determination
And that it would help not to be sour or grumpy
Also, please remind others of our hungry nation.

Inform other people around the globe
Of our stress, dullness, agony and our efforts
Tell them of how we think a feast a glorious show
And of how here, lives hurt.

We envy those who are fortunate and satisfied
Whilst we are cheerless and dull
As each part of their delight and pride
Is a fragment of our miserable soul.

Laura Ewing (11)
Featherby Junior School

CASPER THE CAT

Casper the cat is very fat
He eats like a horse
And sleeps like a bat.
His head's like a football
But he's not very tall
He's got smelly breath
And scares my other puss to death.
His miaow is all squeaky,
He's completely mad
Just like dad!
He smashes the flowerpots
And wrecks all the curtains
And puts his paw in my eye
But he doesn't make me cry.
He pulls the duvet right off me
And I say leave me be!
He's very good at playing
He loves his silver ball
Which he chases up the hall.
But I don't care if he's cheeky because I love him!

Gemma Short (7)
Grove Park CP School

PAIN

A fire inside your heart,
A waterfall in your soul,
Hot inside, all red,
Tears inside, all cold.

Katy Fosbraey (10)
Grove Park CP School

NIGHT

Night
Night is a
Person
A person
Who is kind.
A person who is willing
Just like you and I
Night.

Night
Night is soft,
Night is so calm
Night will never
Harm you
So go on dream
Sweet dreams
She will keep you sleeping
Sleeeeeeeeping,
Snoooooring,
Dreaming.

Zzzzzzzzzzzzzzzz.

Lauren Thrift (10)
Grove Park CP School

LOVE

Love is like a diamond ring,
Like an angel's voice as it sings,
Love is like a hug or kiss,
Love is just like this.

Kellie Jacques (10)
Grove Park CP School

RATACUS RAT

Scamper, scamper,
Round and round
Pitter-patter,
Tappety-tap
Round and round and round.

I'm a rat,
I run from the cat.

Scamper, scamper,
Round and round
Pitter-patter,
Tappety-tap
Round and round and round.

I'm looking for my food,
I'm not in a good mood,
Scamper, scamper,
Round and round
Pitter-patter,
Tappety-tap
Round and round and round.

Hilary James (8)
Grove Park CP School

SUNSHINE

Sunshine glimmers all around
In the air and on the ground.
Sunshine shimmers in the sky
I wish I could touch it but it is too high.

Melanie Hope (9)
Grove Park CP School

FIRST DAY BACK

Monday morning and back to school
After a lazy weekend, it seems so cruel
I haven't done my homework, I'm gonna get done
When I see Mrs Liddon I'll have to run.

It's maths first and a test of division
Now I regret not doing any revision
The lesson is over and it's morning break
I run around and feel wide awake.

English is next and it's silent reading
My tummy's rumbling and quickly needs feeding!
The dinner bell rings and out we run
I scoff my lunch, so I have more time for fun.

Art is next and I have a picture to paint
I finish my work on time, I thought Mrs Liddon would faint!
The school day is over, I run out with my mates
I quickly smile as we pass out the school gates.

Kane Makepeace (9)
Grove Park CP School

MY TRUE FRIEND

Whenever I am lonely,
Whenever I am blue,
Who is always there to cheer me up?
My one true friend is you.

You never try to judge me,
You hear my every word,
You listen when I talk to you
Even when I sound absurd.

You fill my days with laughter,
You fill my heart with joy,
Together we are such good friends
One loyal dog, one boy.

Christopher Shortall (9)
Grove Park CP School

THE SONG OF THE WITCHES

Double, trouble, toil and bubble,
Add some oil at the double.

Eye of snake,
And a rake,
Horrible frog slime,
I think it's time,
To add a bit of lime,
And it'll be fine.

Double, trouble, toil and bubble,
Add some oil at the double.

Stir it round,
On the ground,
Add another wart,
That's what I've been taught,
This one's a winner,
It will make you thinner.

Double, trouble, toil and bubble,
Add some oil at the double.

Sophie Ulyatt (9)
Grove Park CP School

A WIZARD NAMED HARRY POTTER

There is a wizard named Harry Potter
He makes lessons really hotter,
He has two eyes of green,
And he is also very keen.
He has a red, lightning scar,
And the Weasleys have a flying car,
Draco Malfoy is cruel,
Dumbledore really rules,
Harry Potter plays Quidditch,
Harry tries to catch the golden Snitch,
Harry is not lame
He is the master of the game.
Hogwarts is a wizard school
And it is really cool!

Hannah Cheeseman (10)
Grove Park CP School

SNOWMEN

S   ledging children having fun in the snow,
N   o more presents under the tree,
O   mnivores munching at the turkey,
W   e love presents and Christmas.
M   erry Christmas everybody
E   veryone loves crackers,
N   ot Christmas anymore.

Jack Wetherell (8)
Grove Park CP School

MY DOG WIZI

I have a dog
I call him Wizi
He chases his tail
Till he gets dizzy.

I tell him he's a silly pup
But then he's just a little mutt,
He eats his food,
And makes a mess
He really couldn't care less.

I love my dog,
My little Wizi,
Although he puts me in a tizzy,
I love him lots
He's mine forever!

Emma-Rose Ellis (11)
Grove Park CP School

CATS SLEEP ANYWHERE

Cats sleep anywhere
Any table, any chair,
Open drawer, fireplace,
Loads of fur in your face.
On the stair, trip, bang,
In the kitchen goes a clang.
Finely the clanging stops,
And he's had his dinner,
Out the box.

Poppy Davis (10)
Grove Park CP School

MY BIRTHDAY

Hooray, hooray one day to go
Until that time comes to me
It begins with a B
Then i, r, t, h, d, a, y,
Which in my calculations can only spell
Birthday!

Toady's the day it's finally here, when there's a stack of presents sitting
frozen still in the corner of my room
Yippee, yippee which one shall I open first?
Then second?
Then third?
Then fourth?
Then fifth?
Then sixth?
And finally seventh?

Rustle, rustle, rustle, as I shake and shake
Rip, rip, rip off comes the paper
Ahh! Cool,
Ahh! Fantastic,
Ahh! Wicked.

That's my happy birthday!

Robyn Cesary (9)
Grove Park CP School

THE RAINBOW

When the sun meets rain
A rainbow appears
The sight fills me with joy
And chases away my fears.

The colours of the rainbow
Fill the sky
Red, orange, yellow, green, blue, indigo and violet
Way up high.

Stephanie Kenyon (8)
Grove Park CP School

I LOVE TO LEARN

When I go to school on Monday,
It's good to see my friends
I sometimes think to myself
I wish this day would never end.
When I go to school on Tuesday,
It's good to have PE
Running, jumping, skipping, rolling, screaming, shouting yippee.
When I go to school on Wednesday,
It's good to have English,
Reading, writing, spelling tests,
It makes the day the very best.
When I go to school on Thursday,
It's good to have maths,
Adding, subtraction, multiplying,
It makes me feel electrifying.
When I go to school on Friday,
It's good to know today is art,
Painting, drawing, sketching,
I just love taking part.
Now it's time for the weekend,
It's time to have some fun, I say.
Saturday and Sunday I love,
But I'm looking forward to Monday.

Charley Servis (7)
Grove Park CP School

PUPPIES AND DOGS

This is Honey
She's not a toy
She's a fluffy bunny
But isn't a boy.

This is Roofuss
Like a rocket into space
He isn't toothless
And goes at his own pace.

This is Poppy
She's not a flower
She is soppy
But has a lot of power.

This is Winnie
He loves pie
He doesn't know the word tinnie
Actually, neither do I.

I bought these pups together
They were driving me round the bend
I was wondering whether Winnie
Was going to make a friend.

Honey loved Winnie,
Winnie loved Honey,
Honey didn't know the word tinnie
Winnie thought Honey was a fluffy bunny.

Roofuss wasn't that fond of Honey
He was very jealous indeed
The fluffy bunny
Honey just wondered when was her feed.

So they all became friends
Except for Roofuss
So there the story ends
He isn't toothless.

Poppy said bye
And went on her way
She was a bit shy
And came back at the end of the day.

Except for one thing
And just then
An idea ding
They're never going to see each other again.

Sammy Singleton (8)
Grove Park CP School

CHILDREN

Monday's child is very cruel,
Tuesday's child is late for school,
Wednesday's child is good at art,
Thursday's child ate a tart,
Friday's child in a maths test,
Saturday's child heading west,
Sunday's child is making a pie
All the children say good . . .

Bye.

Lee Burke (9)
Grove Park CP School

MY IMAGINARY FRIEND

My imaginary friend
Is lots of fun,
We play a lot of funny games
With costumes and toy guns.

I can see him
No one else can
He is really, really fun
And has a dark tan.
My imaginary friend
Is as fun as fun can be
Although I can see him
He can't see me!

Liam Kenyon (9)
Grove Park CP School

MY UNCLE BART

My Uncle Bart had a funny, old go-kart,
The bits that had stickers on, you could see were painted dark,
Nobody knew what this grand, old go-kart was for,
Although it went round Bayford Meadows for fifty years or more.

It went . . .
Zoom, erchh, crash, ouch, every single day,
Zoom, erchh, crash, ouch, every single day,
Zoom, erchh, crash, ouch, every single day,

The grand, old go-kart.

David Baker (9)
Grove Park CP School

NIGHT

Night makes me feel comforting
He is a kind man
Night is kind and safe, friendly
Night's face is smooth as silk.

His eyes are blue sapphire
Night's lips are as red as ruby
And the ruby is as red as blood.

His hair is like gold, smooth as silk
His clothes are greyish lavender
Dressing like cotton when night moves
I am safe as the moon
When he speaks he makes me feel loved.

He lives in a wooden house
With me
Night and me.

Amy Hanley (10)
Grove Park CP School

FIREWORKS

Fireworks are pretty,
    Fireworks are bright,
I like to watch them as
    They light up the night.
I like the glitter
    Up in the sky
I wish I could reach it
    But it is too high.

Laura Underdown (9)
Grove Park CP School

WONDERFUL WINTER

Cold and frosty winter is very nice to play in
Look at the lovely blanket of white
Oh says everyone that is good
What a good brilliant sight!
Cool, cool, cool, winter is!
Come on everyone let's sing for joy
Oh winter, winter, you're very cold
You're bringing smiles to every girl and boy.
Christmas is very cool, cool and cool
Winter is good, good, good
Oh Christmas and winter you're both very cold
So why don't we celebrate with a bit of Christmas pud!

Rachel Foulger (8)
Grove Park CP School

MY CAT MAISY

My cat Maisy likes to sit
Among the daisies she will sit there for hours
Until the clouds turn to showers.
If she gets wet she might go to the vet
For she might have a cold or the flu.
Back home in the warm
She will snuggle and yawn
For now it is time for her bed.
Goodnight sweet Maisy
While I stroke your sweet head.

Mia Harbour (10)
Grove Park CP School

SUMMER

The sun is shining bright
My skirt is a bit too tight
My mum is a little bit hot
Then my dad smashed a pot.
The sand was yellow
The sea was shallow
The birds were singing lovely
Then my sister dropped her dummy.
My nan dropped a pan
My brother's name is Dan
My friend has a cat
It sleeps on a mat.

Rachelle Grubb (8)
Grove Park CP School

WINTER'S WAYS

Snowballs flying in the winter breeze,
Night-time freezing with an icy breeze,
Old owls hooting in the willow trees,
We are having little snowy dreams
And snowmen standing by the winter trees.
Night-time breeze flowing through the willow trees
Getting ready for the winter snow.
Eating turkey that smells so delicious
Snowmen just standing on my door step
And that's the end of my poem.

Sennen Thrift (8)
Grove Park CP School

HOCUS POCUS

Fizzy wizzy,
Crackle and pop,
Frogs' legs,
Beans and monkey thumbs,
Mouldy peas and mouldy plums,
Pickled eyes and scaly tongues.

Poisonous dips,
Squashed flies,
Sizzled bees and mud pies,
Seaweed,
Keys,
Ribbon, bows,
Smelly feet and ice cream cones.

Spider stew and snake brains,
Horses' tails and
Elephants' ears,
Donkeys' hooves,
Fresh green grass,
Gone off tea and
Yellow fluff.

Fizzy wizzy,
Crackle and pop,
Frogs' legs,
Beans and monkey thumbs,
Mouldy peas and mouldy plums,
Pickled eyes and scaly tongues.

Jasmine Ives (9)
Grove Park CP School

WINTER WONDERLAND

Winter wonderland is a great place to go
There is ice and lots of snow.

Winter wonderland is a great place to be
There are lots of wonderful sights to see.

Winter wonderland is a great place
It has lots of room and space.

Winter wonderland is a great sight
It goes all through the day and all through the night.

When we go that's not so bad,
So you don't have to be sad,
Because you will always be in winter wonderland.

Winter wonderland!

Tazreen Beasley (8)
Grove Park CP School

SNOW FUN

A snowman I will build
He might even have a shield.
Snowball fights I will play
All through night and day.
Snowflakes fall from the sky
And when the sun comes out,
They will melt away and say goodbye.
How am I going to play in the snow tomorrow?
I wish I could borrow today for tomorrow.

Rachel Foreman (9)
Grove Park CP School

SLEDGING

S nowman standing in a blanket of snow
L ights on the tree, blazing by the fire
E merald green decorations attacking the light blue
D ancing all night, playing in the snow
G oing for the pudding after the Christmas dinner for a happy
midnight cheer!
  Everyone saying 'Will he come?' Mother says 'Of course not,
you've not been good.'
I nto bed early on Christmas Eve
N ight is dawning on Christmas Eve
'G reat, it's Christmas Day.'

Alastair Rushworth (7)
Grove Park CP School

YOUNG MAN

There was a young man
Who did nothing but read, read, read
Except at breakfast, lunch and dinner
When he did nothing but feed, feed, feed.
His mum and dad said he was too fat
His problem was greed, greed, greed.
Reading and eating, not running about
Soon he was dead, dead, dead.

Sophie Rowlinson-Rogers (8)
St William Of Perth RC Primary School, Rochester

THIS IS A SPECIAL DAY

I was sailing on my wooden ship
Exploring for this wonderful treasure
When the violent waves made my boat tip
Then I found that this journey was lacking in pleasure.

    This is an infrequent day.

Through the mysterious, misty fog I sailed
Still waiting for the storm to go
Then the gloomy, dull sky wailed
While this was happening the mist got very low.

    This is an infrequent day.

The sea was jittering,
The sky was grey,
The stars were wittering,
The fishes were so bored they had to play.

    This is an infrequent day.

I go down deep
I float around
Down I go
Down! Down! Down!

    This is an infrequent day.

I'm down now
I'm right to the bottom
All I need now is the amazing treasure
I've seen something but is this the treasure?

Yes it is!
I've found the amazing treasure!

Gemma Kitchenham (10)
Senacre Wood Primary School

THE WAY TO THE TREASURE

At the bottom of the sea
Is where the treasure will be
Protected by Mother Nature.
The unstoppable waves,
Are the thunderstorm's slaves.

In the land of the Turks
Is where the treasure lurks
Protected by Mother Nature.
Sharks in a swarm
A circle they form.

Not high in the air
The treasure isn't there,
Protected by Mother Nature.
Not up in the clouds.
Not down on the ground.

So be careful and a rich man you'll be.

Jordan Clarke (11)
Senacre Wood Primary School

HIDDEN TREASURES

There I was staring underwater for gold so I put
My scuba diving clothes on and I was just about
To dive in the sea just at the last minute.

I went and asked my dad please, please let's find gold
Or green diamonds please, please, let me find silver or bronze and gold
I did not
I feel trepidation.

'You're going to be alright, we have gold already!'
I was discombobalted when he said we have got some gold
We saw a golden crow
It looked timid.

Tyo Williams (11)
Senacre Wood Primary School

THE WAY TO RICHES

The way to riches is to discover the treasure
Lost in the middle of this island
When I find it my life will be a pleasure
The treasure's in the centre of this island.

Venomous green snakes, rough, red lions and ghostly crocodiles
Lie in my dangerous path.
I'll even walk painfully for miles
The treasure's in the middle of this island.

There'll be riddles such as
What's the middle of middle and the end of end,
My second's in crystal, but not in jewel
My final's in money, but not in honey
The treasure will be past the?

Following the clue
Leads to my precious prize
Never shall I be blue.
I'll find the treasure in the centre of this island.

Felicity Bax (11)
Senacre Wood Primary School

THE HIDDEN TREASURES

Hidden treasures I just had found
At the bottom of the blue ocean,
All I thought it would be was just a couple of pounds,
Or would I turn out rich.

Something is guarding it
I could just about see,
An octopus' pit
And it's not very happy, it's seen me.

I knew I shouldn't risk the tusk
And it wasn't just the octopus
There's a shark
So I didn't do it.

I knew I would miss the treasure
I knew I could get what I wanted,
But if I did have it, it would bring me lots of pleasure
Maybe I'll regret it.

Bethanie Jones (10)
Senacre Wood Primary School

BELOW THE SEA I SAW . . .

As I was below the sea
The golden fish and me
I saw a big grey cave
Was it me or was I brave?

I went closer and closer
And deeper and deeper
Until I got to the ground
And swam along and I found.

A bony skeleton with a ruby eye
With a key around its neck I will try
I finally got it and opened the cave
'I've done it, I've done it!' and cor was I brave!

Sophie Boatman (11)
Senacre Wood Primary School

HIDDEN TREASURE

I was sitting on my old boat one day
When suddenly I saw
Something sparkling in my eyes
I'd never seen before.

So I jumped off my boat
And dived in the sea,
I swam so fast,
Thinking what could it be?

As I got closer,
I could see it on a rock,
It was the hidden treasure
Trapped inside by a huge lock.

I found a key beside it
And I put it in the lock
I twisted it around
Inside was a golden clock!

This was the ancient, golden clock
That I had been looking for
And now that I've found it
I am no longer poor.

Kirsty Milner (11)
Senacre Wood Primary School

At The Bottom Of The Sea

At the bottom of the sea
Where a large treasure chest lay
There were ten hungry sharks looking out for tea
And all the treasure was at Bombay Bay.

All the divers that have been there
Have never been seen since,
But some say that one boy just survived the share
Of the ten hungry sharks munching on some mince.

Who was this boy?
Some say his name's Terry,
Some say it's Roy
And some say it might be Perry.

But who knows?
Only one boy
Because the boy who knows
Is old, boy Troy.

Shaun Whiffen (10)
Senacre Wood Primary School

Down In The Deep Depths Of The Sea

The mariner was clawed by a raging, hissing cat
Guarding the treasures at the bottom of the sea
But something deadlier lies there still
Down in the deep depths of the sea.

A skull, staring with emerald-green eyes,
Guarding the treasures at the bottom of the sea
With a starfish for a nose, a jellyfish for hair,
Down in the deep depths of the sea.

Its teeth are a rotted yellow, jagged yet flint-like
Guarding the treasures at the bottom of the sea,
Uneven holes scattered over the defaced skull,
Down in the deep depths of the sea.

Lucy Stratton (11)
Senacre Wood Primary School

HIDDEN TREASURE

When the spotlight passed his lips
We knew we would find treasure
We went through the hard way
Through the big pink ears.

> We travelled through the candle wax
> And around the jelly maze
> Through the noisy studio
> Followed with a daze.

We were whisked away by a bright stream
And taken far away
Through a valentine's picture
And a greyish, scary prison.

> We reached the end of our journey
> A funny food shop
> Where all the food was eaten
> With all rotten food on top.

So this was the treasure
A lump of food
What a waste of time
Now I wished I had followed the milk bottles!

Amy Boatman (11)
Senacre Wood Primary School

MY MIND IS PRECIOUS

I travelled inside my own smart head
To find four doors in my own little head
One said feelings and one said brain
Another said imagination and another said how to go insane.

I thought and thought in my own smart head
And took door number four in my own head,
Inside were flying stars
And a giant Mars bar.

I decided not to go insane in my own smart head
But I wanted to go back to my unfair life
To see my imaginary children and imaginary wife.

A man in a bright blue suit came to me in my own little head
He said that I won the golden prize
But it wasn't gold, it was my golden memories,
That's my most precious treasure of all.

Jayleigh Nicholson (10)
Senacre Wood Primary School

MYSTICAL MAGIC

Down at the bottom of the ocean
I was surrounded by shiny shimmering jewels
Which shone as the bright sun spoke to them
There were necklaces which had lovely sparkling jewels in them
Queen's rings with silver crystals.

They were speaking to me
They'd never seen a human before
I quickly and quietly took the little treasures
I said to myself they are the best little things.

Gemma Smith (10)
Senacre Wood Primary School

HIDDEN TREASURES

I jump right into my golden submarine
I couldn't wait for my adventure to begin
The deep sea, so wonderful nested with fish and seaweed
And a shark just swimming with its gleaming, sharp teeth.

I look in caves, in seaweed and in shipwrecks too
And all I find is a couple of old sharks.
No clues to help me on my journey so deep
Ahh! I remember my friend who gave me a clue.

Follow the big, purple octopus then you'll find your riches
So I did just that and on the way I saw a catfish and a shark too
But no octopus, some clue.

Then I saw it, just in the distance, on top of a chest
And right I was it was the treasure box, not looking at its best
I grabbed the chest and zoomed to the surface bed
Feeling quite relieved I made it back, all that money's hurting my head!

Daniel Tucker (10)
Senacre Wood Primary School

THE HIDDEN TREASURE

It's hidden away under the Caribbean Sea
Among the golden, blond sand
In all the slimmer seaweed and the grass-green bushes
It's hidden away under the Caribbean Sea.

It's guarded by sharks with white, sparkling teeth
And their spicker tails with one quick slash will knock you dead
Their eyes turn like fire when people come down
It's hidden away under the Caribbean Sea.

Emma Russell (11)
Senacre Wood Primary School

WHERE'S HIDDEN TREASURE HIDDEN?

It's in the garden, up a tree
But where in the garden can it be?

It's in the shed, under a car
But where in the shed can it be?

It's in the cupboard or at the bottom of the sea
But where in the cupboard can it be?

It's on the shelf, that's where you will find it
But what shelf can it be?

The top one is where you will find it.

Terry Simmons (11)
Senacre Wood Primary School

THE HIDDEN TREASURES

I found this place with hidden treasures, emeralds and radiant coins
This sequestered place, solitary like my home
With mermaids, eels and fish
The dejection hit me, like one thousand knives as like I didn't matter.

I found this place with hidden treasures, emeralds and radiant coins
My soul surrounded me
My heart haunted me!
But in my mind it was worth the hidden treasures,
                                    emeralds and radiant coins!

Jack Maxwell (11)
Senacre Wood Primary School

LOST TREASURE

I looked up in a book one day
And found what was to me
A book of hidden treasure
At the bottom of the sea.

I set off for my journey
Through weather hot or cold
I was fierce, ancient and keen
I knew I wouldn't hold.

At night I would dream of all the glory
With all my pot of gold
I knew I would become
The greatest lord of the world.

I dived into the bottom of the sea
To find what was to me
The greatest treasure of them all
I found a golden key.

Emma Winter (10)
Senacre Wood Primary School

LOST TREASURE

Shiny treasure where are you?
Under a rock or under the sea?
In my head or in a boat?
My head is buzzing like a bee.

Shiny treasure where are you?
Upon the sand or by the sea?
Maybe you're floating on the shore
Perhaps I'll see you next time.

Jessica Barber (11)
Senacre Wood Primary School

HIDDEN BODY TREASURE

Whoosh!
Up the gooey nostril I go.

Exploring for shimmering treasure.

In and out the strings
Out the voice box it sings.

Exploring for shimmering treasure.

This is like a bouncy castle
Here comes down a watery parcel.

Exploring for shimmering treasure.

Down the rebounding arm I go
The thumping, pumping blood that flows.

Exploring for shimmering treasure.

Climbing up the great arm again
Gushing food like a whip of a cane.

Exploring for shimmering treasure.

'Och, eek, oi' land
Smack! Wait a minute this feels like sand.

Exploring for shimmering treasure.

No, this is not
It is such a big pot.

Inside was . . .
    Treasure!

Kerry Mason (10)
Senacre Wood Primary School

FINDING VALUABLES

Deep beneath the timid sea
Where the fishes play happily
Underneath the true blue sea
The dolphins shout 'Come with me.'
As I get closer, I gradually behold,
A treasure chest, that's very old.

I find a diamond key and the captain follows me
To find a secret treasure chest
Inside I find a freight of treasure
That I've never ever caught sight of.

Lia Josling (11)
Senacre Wood Primary School

DO I HAVE TO GO TO SCHOOL, MUM?

Do I have to go to school, Mum?
It's really just not fair.
The teachers make us work and work,
Until our brains are bare.
Do I have to go to school, Mum?
I really feel quite ill,
I just can't face another day,
I think I'm going to run away.
Do I have to go to school, Mum?
Why is it me, not you?
I know I'm not going to do my best.
Why don't you let me have a rest?

Eleanor Webb (11)
Shernold School

KITTY AND PUP

Kitty and Pup were up one morning
Eating breakfast too.
Kitty said, 'Let's play in the muck
And get all muddy too.'
Pup got his squeaky bone
And Kitty got her chew.
They all climbed a tree and said,
'Peek-a-boo!'

Kirsty Keep (8)
Shernold School

THE PAPERCLIP

Squish the paper
Squeeze it tight,

Let the paper go loose
Let the paperclip fly,

'Yes, I am free,' said the paperclip,
He bounced and he pounced.

Lydia Jakob-Grant (10)
Shernold School

COLOUR GREEN

Colour green
as green as the grass
like the swaying trees
in the garden.

Green for the leaves
on our rose trees
that we see in the park
as we pass.

Elora Williams (9)
Shernold School

Teachers

Some teachers are mean
Some teachers are cruel
Some teachers are clever
Some teachers are cool
Some teachers are evil
Some teachers are small
Some teachers are slim
Some teachers are tall
At our school we have
Got 'em all.

Jade Waymouth (10)
Shernold School

Animals

A   ardvark feeds on ants
N   aughty elephants splash in water
I   nsects are small animals like ants
M   ammals are like humans
A   anteaters live on ants
L   eopards have spots
S   nakes are slimy.

Rebecca Reardon (8)
Shernold School

MY PUDDY-TATS!

My cats' names are
Thunder and Lightning,
Even though their names are tough
They're not that rough.
They're even scared of thunder and lightning
When it comes!
Thunder is very silly
He falls down about two stairs!
Lightning on the other hand
Is afraid to jump.
When we hear him miaow
We *have* to go and rescue him from a table.
Even though one is silly and one is scared
I love them both . . . so
Hands off, they're mine!

Lexy Payne (9)
Shernold School

FRIENDS

F riends are great - make new, keep old.
R emembering the good times and sad times.
I love friends, just everybody has got one.
E xploring our secrets with them.
N ever let them down.
D oing things with them is fun.
S o never, never break up.

Grace Stanford (9)
Shernold School

MY SISTER

My sister has brown eyes,
and brown hair too,
she kind of looks a bit like me too.
People say she's really sweet,
but I would rather have something to eat.
She is always calling my name,
saying, 'Can we play a game?'
Her favourite food is pasta or rice,
she thinks they taste really nice.
I suppose she's not that bad,
even when she drives me mad.
I like her being around,
my little sister Sophie.

Victoria Webb (10)
Shernold School

MY HOBBY

H orse riding is fun
O ver the jumps
R eins, I hold tightly
S tirrups for my feet to grip
E mma is my riding teacher

R ising trot around the ring
I love riding Benny
D onna, I love to ride as well
I n the stables, there is lots to do
N icely groomed for the show
G razing in the field.

Harriett Cowen (8)
Shernold School

WHAT AM I?

Am I a horse
That gallops all day?

Am I a monkey
That swings through the trees?

Am I giraffe
As tall as the sky?

Am I a blue whale
That swims in the sea?

Am I a person
Who goes to school?

Yes, that's me.

Ellie-Bliss Chirnside (11)
Shernold School

JAKE

Hi, I'm a black and white cat
and my name is Jake,
I jump up and down on the garden gate.

I watch the birds and rabbits too,
but never catch anything
because I'm fat and slow.

I live in a small house
in the middle of Kent
and I love all the fields and hills and scent.

Jenny Cosgrove (9)
Shernold School

THE OWL

Every night,
The owl takes flight,
It glides through the air,
Landing with care,
The moon full and grey,
The owl seeking prey.
As it gazes,
Ambitions blazes,
It's seen a mouse,
Heading for its house,
The owl swoops down,
It finally caught it,
Though you wouldn't have thought it.

Rebecca Harris (10)
Shernold School

JANUARY

January is a month of wind, rain and snow,
Sometimes leaving us with nowhere to go,
Stormy wind making trees bow over,
Rain falling from London to Dover,
Then the snow falls down on us,
Is it deep enough to stop a bus?
Although we might catch a cold,
And leaves us feeling rather old,
It doesn't stop us from having fun,
Although we don't have any sun.

Harriet Massie (9)
Shernold School

CHOCOLATE

Chocolate is delicious,
Chocolate is nice,
Chocolate is irresistible,
Even with rice.

Chocolate is brown,
Chocolate is white,
Chocolate is chunky,
Chocolate is light.

Chocolate is milky,
Chocolate is sticky,
Chocolate is gorgeous,
Chocolate is a delight.

Christina Mo (8)
Shernold School

MY PET GUINEA PIG

My pet guinea pig has ears,
I never, ever see him in tears.
He eats and sleeps day and night,
I don't even see him fight.
He eats and eats so greedily,
I don't even see him do a wee.
He plays with his friends until nine,
I even sometimes hear him whine.
Although he has no human stuff or a wig,
I will always love my little guinea pig.

Abigail Pile (8)
Shernold School

HOW I LOVE MY CAT

How I love playing with my cat
Every day when I get home from school

If I get a piece of string and pull it across the ground
He will chase it and drag it around.

How I love to watch him staring at the TV
But if something boring is on he will come and get me
And we will play hide-and-seek.
Of course he always wins
Because he knows so many places.

When we hear the Simpsons on the TV
We will rush back to our places
And then watch TV
And that's the way I like to be.

Isabelle Loader (9)
Shernold School

DIDDLEY, THE DOG

Whenever I go anywhere
People stop and stare.
They're not trying to be mean
They've never seen a dog so green.
I've got a brother who is blue
But a lot, lot younger.
So if anyone stops and stares
He will bring a lot of thunder.

Bethany Gerrish (8)
Shernold School

BOOKS

You look at books from an early age,
Though you can't read the words written on the page.

As you get older you figure it out,
You understand what the words are about.

Once you can read life becomes fun,
There're plenty of books to please everyone.

Whatever your interest, whatever you do
You'll find a book that will suit you.

Reference books help you learn
How things grow and how things burn.

What happened in Victorian times,
How to do maths and draw straight lines.

Best of all are books to read
For pleasure, when you've had your tea.

Harry Potter's my favourite book,
If you haven't read it, take a look!

Abby Savage (10)
Shernold School

CHOCOLATE

Chocolate, chocolate, really sweet
Chocolate, chocolate, my favourite thing to eat!
The taste of chocolate's really yummy,
It goes all tingly in my tummy.
But don't eat too much or you will get fat!
And that . . . is that.

Bethany Sidwell (10)
Shernold School

THE COLDEST SWIMMING POOL IN THE WORLD!

The coldest swimming pool is in Egypt,
You really, really couldn't believe it.
Egypt is hot
But the swimming pool's not.
It freezes your toes
And bites your nose.
It found bits of Mummy she never knew she had
But I don't think it's all that bad
And dad wouldn't even try it!

I swam and swam
My heart went bam, bam.
When I got out
You should hear me shout.
Boy, that swimming pool's cold!
Don't go in it I told.

Alexandra Browne (8)
Shernold School

DON'T WAVE YOUR HAND ABOUT

'Don't wave your hand about,' the teacher said.
If he thinks we'll take off he hasn't a brain cell in his head.
Then he suddenly said what I was thinking,
And it was then when I felt my heart sinking.
'You will take off in a minute,' he says.
When I've finished with him it'll be the end of his days.
I'll shoot him with a bazooka twice,
But no, I couldn't do that 'cause I'm too nice.

Eleanor Oliver (9)
Shernold School

CHOCOLATE

Yum, yum, chocolate
Sitting on the side
All wrapped up
With gooey toffee inside.

Just one bit
Mum won't know
I'll still eat my tea
So it won't show.

Mmm, tastes so good
I'll have another
Just one more
And another and another.

Oh, three bits left
I'll have to eat them quick
I hope no one notices
But now I feel quite sick.

Jessica Rogers (9)
Shernold School

KARATE

You punch,
You kick,
But there is no gain
If there is no pain!
The teacher's called Sensei
But when I catch his eye
All I see is him looking at me
And shouting, *'Dai!'*
I love karate!

Cara Heffernan (10)
Shernold School

MY PET, LUCKY

Lucky is a rabbit
As black as the night
He is cute and cuddly
He never does bite
He lives in the kitchen
In a bright blue cage
If there's a book on the floor
He chews up the page
He follows you around
Wherever you go
He licks you all over
From head to toe
I've never met a rabbit
Quite like Lucky
But I know one thing
He makes me very happy.

Michaela Savage (8)
Shernold School

MY OLD NEIGHBOURS

My old neighbours are the best I've had,
They more like a surrogate mum and dad.
They take me places I like to go,
If I ask for something they hardly ever say no.
I've known them ever since I was four years old,
I didn't know what to say to them when my house was sold.
The day I left I said goodbye,
She gave me a kiss and I was about to cry.

Grace Rudgard (10)
Shernold School

DANCING

I like dancing
because you get to do shows.
I do ballroom
and wear lovely clothes.

Disco when you wear sparkly clothes
And sparkles in your eyes.
We wiggle our bums
And shake our thighs.

My favourite is ballroom
I like the fast pace.
Jive, quickstep and the Cha-Cha-Cha
And some trip over their shoelace.

Lauren Smith (9)
Shernold School

FORMULA ONE

Burn lots of rubber, use lots of fuel.
Lights go green, Murray shouts, 'Go, go, go!'
The crowds roar and off you go.
The car twists and turns as you speed round the track.
Into the pit to refuel in seconds.
Out you go to regain your position.
As you pass the chequered flag in pole position.
The trophy you get will celebrate your glory.

George Edwardes (9)
Shernold School

MY DRAGON

I have a little pet dragon
Who sleeps at the bottom of my bed
He is always very happy
Especially when he is fed.

I call my pet dragon Harry
And he is my best friend
But sometimes he is naughty
Which drives me round the bend.

Harry's colours are red and green
And he is rough to touch
But even when he is being bad
I still love him very much.

Megan Rumball (8)
Shernold School

MY FRIEND

My friend is very beautiful,
She likes me very much.
She's the bestest friend in the whole wide world,
She's never fierce enough.

She has a brother and lots of friends,
I don't always see her very much.
She does games at Brownies
And sewing and cooking too,
She likes to play with me a lot.

Shelby-Jo Bellamy (8)
Shernold School

SPIKE

Spike is my cat
I love him so
He has three legs
But he's still raring to go.

Spike is white
With yellow eyes
I cuddle him tight
Whenever he cries.

He likes me to pat his head
He likes to curl up on my bed
He's so special it's plain to see
I'm so glad he lives with me.

Jessica Moss (11)
Shernold School

CHRISTMAS

Christmas is a time to share,
And help each other here and there.
A time to put the decorations up,
Then eat the Christmas pudding.
A time to get the Christmas tree,
A time to see your families.
It's a time to think of Jesus Christ,
A time to think about children in need.
We sing songs to people at their house,
We hope Jesus is happy in the sky,
As He flies.

Nancy Watts (8)
Shernold School

THE DISCOVERY

In hot and sandy Egypt,
On the banks of the Nile
You see the ancient pyramids
A sight to make you smile.

In the Valley of the Kings
Amongst the sand and rock
Hide the tombs of pharaohs
Their discovery was a shock.

One day, Howard Carter
Found a load of gold.
The tomb of Tutankhamun
A wonderful sight to behold.

William Lay (8)
Shernold School

THINGS I LIKE TO DO

I like doing swimming and to splash,
I get to the other end in a flash.
I enjoy gymnastics,
Because I am very elastic.
I like to dance around
Because I like to get my feet off the ground.
I like to play my recorder
Because I can get the notes in the right order.
I like to play on my scooter
Because it does not have a hooter.

Lesley Connor (8)
Shernold School

MY DOG PRINCE

My dog, Prince, is the best dog ever,
He's half mad and he's half clever.
He's only 9 months old, and he's a golden Labrador,
And sometimes when he goes to bed he begins to snore.
He follows you around when you're holding his food,
But he doesn't bite when he's in a mood.
He jumps up at you and licks you on the face,
And when he's crazy he runs all over the place.
Sometimes he makes a mess by chewing up a log,
But even though he does all this he's still the world's best dog.

Lourdes Webb (9)
Shernold School

GINGER, MY HAMSTER

My hamster, Ginger, he is so cute
He's from Siberia, what a beaut.

Dad cleans his cage out every week
He's hard to catch and makes a squeak.

He crawls around his cage at night
During the day he's out of sight.

He's everything a hamster should be
I am so glad he lives with me.

Olivia Moss (9)
Shernold School

LION

A roaring noise from the trees,
Loud, large and fearsome,
Bouncing off the trees.

A swishing tail swaying closer and closer,
Trudging through the undergrowth,
Snapping twigs, rustling leaves.

Ever more closer,
Closer it comes,
Ever more closer.

Gleaming malicious eyes,
Peering through the branches,
Looking for suitable prey.

A torso from the trees,
Large and hairy,
Entering the clearing.

A set of legs,
Patrolling the forest grounds,
Enter King Lion of the forest floor.

Clare Stally (11)
Sherwin Knight School

RAIN FALLS

Rain falls heavily
As sharp as small, little pins
A thunderstorm comes.

Charlotte O'Brien (11)
Sherwin Knight School

NATURE

Nature is like a forest at night,
Lots of different animals come out from the underground,
While birds wrap up tight,
Listen to the badgers' rustling sound.

Nature is like a rainforest in the morning,
The birds watching as the leaves are falling,
The badgers hurry home,
And you can hear the owls moan.

Nature has lots of sounds in the air,
The scuttling of the hare,
The singing of the birds,
And sometimes a deer herd.

Annie Edwards (9)
Sherwin Knight School

THE KITTEN

I met a kitten in my room
As I was sweeping with my broom.
I looked at the cat
He was very fat.
I gave it some food
But he was very rude
And turned his back
And I gave it a whack.
At the end of the day
He said, 'You'll pay.'
Then ran off home all alone.

Daniel Gardner (10)
Sherwin Knight School

LEOPARD

Fast runner
Meat eater
Brilliant hider
High pouncer
Fierce eater
Body swiper
Human killer
Fast mover.

Karissa Bristow (10)
Sherwin Knight School

ME AND MY DAD

My dad and me are good at games
I help him and he helps me.
He's up for the challenge
He's really cool.
He's my favourite person
He's the best for me and I love him lots.
He's my special dad.

Daniel Andrews (10)
Sherwin Knight School

DAVID BECKHAM

He scores all the goals with rage.
He runs like a hyena.
He plays for great teams.
He has lots of crazy haircuts.
He is a hero to me.

Jake Chapman (10)
Sherwin Knight School

CAT

Mouse catcher
Ball chaser
People pouncer
Wall biter
Rubbish ripper
Wood scratcher
Fast runner.

Lucy Buckle (10)
Sherwin Knight School

MY RABBIT

He jumps for happiness.
He is filled with life.
He loves to be rubbed.
He is as kind as a fly.
He is as fluffy as can be.
He is a true friend to me.

Holly MacDonald-Heaney (10)
Sherwin Knight School

BOYFRIEND

Boyfriend loves you lots.
He loves being romantic.
He is the cutest.
When I met him he was great.
I will never forget him.

Tessa Marshall (10)
Sherwin Knight School

ZEBRA

Water licker
Ear raiser
Colour clencher
Hero trainer
Child protector
Fast runner
Heart pounder
Tender lover.

Jade Buckley (10)
Sherwin Knight School

DRAGON

Bone cruncher
Heart burner
Giant eater
Fire blower
Blood drinker
Flesh digger
Claw swiper
Belly burner.

Luke Fauklin (11)
Sherwin Knight School

SHADOWS

Shadows passing by
The gentle blow going past you
Quietly gliding, without sound.

Charlotte Ashdown (11)
Sherwin Knight School

MY MUM

She is as kind as my dad.
She is as thin as a book.
She is taller than me.
Her hair is as brown as a tree.
Her hands are as clean as a white board.
Her eyes are as blue as the sea.
Her face is like a butterfly's wings.

Samantha Louise Francis (10)
Sherwin Knight School

SOUND WORD POEM

The whistle of birds
Singing up in the trees.
The bang of guns
Shooting in the breeze.
The sound of a tap dripping
All day long.

Tuncay Albay (9) & Jordan Wright (8)
Sherwin Knight School

ABOUT MY CAT

My cat is funny.
She likes going out when it is sunny.
She is called Mitsy but I call her Sissy.
My cat is very tiny and very tidy.
And I love her.

Charlie Tullett (9)
Sherwin Knight School

MY MUMMY

She is as kind as ant running on the road.
She is as red as a rose.
She is as pretty as the queen.
She is as loving as the world all together
She is as soft as a flower petal in the sun.
She is as helpful as a waiter in a restaurant.
She is a cuddly teddy.
She is a hot water bottle.
    She is my mummy.

Alex Stanley (10)
Sherwin Knight School

MY BEDROOM

My purple bedroom,
It's so bright and colourful.
It shines like a star.
It is the best room so far.
I am so happy in there.

Sherry Kay (10)
Sherwin Knight School

DANCERS

Great smiler
Fast spinner
Clever jumper
Eye catcher.

Racheal Noble (11)
Sherwin Knight School

DEEP IN THE JUNGLE

Deep in the jungle,
Tall trees above the clouds,
Grass as long as sunflower seeds.

A roaring noise behind the foliage,
A trunk like a piece of old rope
Peers from behind large leaves,
Reaching up high for food.

Large, grey ears flap against he wind,
Listening, listening to see if any hunters are about.

One huge leg thumps out from the bushes,
The gigantic greyness,
A giant stamps from the trees.

Laura Howse (10)
Sherwin Knight School

LOLLY STICK

Alex, Alex, Alex
Lick, Lick, Lick, go
Qwick, gwick, gwick
On the lolly stick
Before it gets nicked
It's melting
I'm sweltering
Now hurry!
I'm going to tell my mummy
Oh no! It's fallen off
I told you it's going to fall.

Liza Smith (9)
Sherwin Knight School

PARENTS

As little children, parents are our best friends
And we love them very much
We don't need any other friends
And when I cuddle them it makes my fingers clutch

A few years later

They don't like my friends
They never let me stay out at night
They treat me like a baby
They say I'll get into a fight

My parents are so bossy
They cause me lots of mayhem
As I get older I worry
That I will be just like them.

Natalie Georgiou (10)
Sherwin Knight School

THE SOFT DOG!

I'm sitting in the chair watching TV,
The door opens,
It's coming through the door,
Its nose twitches in and out,
Its tail wriggles in delight at seeing me,
The teeth sharp but blunt to bite,
Its paws jumping on to me,
The dog is cosy.

Lucy Naish (10)
Sherwin Knight School

PEAS AND CHIPS

I hate peas,
They wobble my knees.
Everyone here hates peas.
Peas, peas, peas, peas, peas.
They always make me sneeze.
Peas wobble my knees
And always make me sneeze.

Chips, chips, much, much better.
Everyone here loves them old chips.
They taste like a Twix.
Chips, chips, chips, chips, chips.
They put me in a mix.
Chips taste like a Twix
And they put me in a mix.

Kyle Collins (10)
Sherwin Knight School

KILLER WOLF

Fangs ripping out the flesh,
Eyes black, piercing, dangerous,
A wet, rough, mean nose,
Ears flapping powerfully and viciously,
The legs - strong, deadly legs,
Running quickly after prey,
Clawing with long, sharp daggers.
It's heading for me.
Furiously the wolf!

Kelly Pike (11)
Sherwin Knight School

Bart The Bat

In the zombie's heart
That was in parts
There sat
A scary bat
And its name is Bart.

Becky Anne Bell (8)
Sherwin Knight School

Wayne The Pain

There once was a boy called Wayne
Who really was a pain
He had a house
He had a mouse
And was never seen again.

Megan Emily Bowne (8)
Sherwin Knight School

Fat Cat

Once there was a fat, fat cat
Who sat on his big, big mat
He saw an ant
And began to pant
And he hit it with a bat.

Bethany Riddle (8)
Sherwin Knight School

CRAZY DAISY

There was a girl called Daisy,
Who was enormously lazy,
All she did,
Was suck a lid,
She was incredibly crazy.

Kiera Mae Butler (8)
Sherwin Knight School

RAINBOW

Colours of the world
Shooting over the bright sky.
Rainbows are lovely
Just heaven, God's world above.
An archway of love and peace.

Ashley Mark Stanley (11)
Sherwin Knight School

STRANGE BELL

There once was a bell that went dong,
Which sang a funny song,
It went ding,
Then it went ring,
Then it went really wrong.

Alexander Stephen Lane (9)
Sherwin Knight School

BIKE!

Mum, can I have a bike?
The colour should be orange,
With cool writing down the side,
With thick, blue rubber bits.

Well, it is my birthday!
There is nothing else I want.
You'll see how cool it is. *Please!*
I'm sure I will get one.

Yippee! It's my birthday.
There is a box on the table.
I open it up and find?
My bike! Yippee! Great!

Lewis Herring (10)
Sherwin Knight School

SOUND WORD POEMS

The woooooo of the wind
Growling all night.
The t toooooo of the owl
Cuddling up tight.
The vrmm vrmm of my dad's car
Going to buy a saw.
The squidge of the mud
As I step out the door.

Matthew Pamflett & Kierran Boden (9)
Sherwin Knight School

MY BEDROOM

My room's messy, but only a little bit,
It looks like a bomb has hit it,
It's funny because it looks like my bunny,
Who has a great big dummy.

My door is full of posters,
Which are all about Zola,
Zola likes coasters,
Which are sponsored by Gola.

My boxes are overflowing,
Because I keep on going,
To the shops,
And keep on getting stuff off Cyclops.

Alex Potter (10)
Sherwin Knight School

COLOURS

Peach is a creamy colour, as soft as silk
And a baby's bottom when it's drinking milk.

Red is a ball of fire
The colour of someone's desire.

Green is the colour of the world
The colour of nature.

Gold is valuable
But not like people.

Colours are all around us!

Sarah Chohan (10)
Sherwin Knight School

MY CAT

Missy is a mess
And very cute, she's very tiny too.
She can be funny and smells like honey.
She has sharp claws like a fierce dragon
And likes playing with money.

She is very cuddly
And very muddly.
Suddenly she gets into a bad mood.
She's black and kind of brown
And her face is very round.

If you take her to the park
She scares all the dogs.
Then the dogs being to bark.
When you bring her back
She stretches out on her mat.

Leah Deaves (10)
Sherwin Knight School

THE WAY IT USED TO BE

I like the magic number 3,
The way it used to be.
When 1 was mum
And 2 was dad
And 3 was little old me.

But 1 is growing fat and round
And 2 waits at the door,
So here's me counting to the magic number 4.

Kirsty Lou Mayle (10)
Sherwin Knight School

THE BEACH

I tread through sandy beaches,
I end up in the sea,
There I see dolphins,
Diving down to the ocean bed.
Among the breeze,
Blows the sand.
Among the forest trees,
Nature lies calm and still.
It turns to dark,
And sunset comes,
A lovely golden sky.
There it shines amongst the sand,
And the forest trees.

Victoria Watson (10)
Sherwin Knight School

FOOTBALL

My shirt over my head
Orange and blue with golden stars
Black, shiny boots
Blue shorts, a bit too long.

I'm ready to go
I warm up on the pitch
Jogging, stretching, shooting
I'm ready to play
The ref blows the whistle
Off we go.

We win!

Michael Wright (9)
Sherwin Knight School

MY MUM

She is a big, cuddly teddy bear,
She is a best friend to me.
She is a funny cheetah,
She is a warm blanket.
She is a smooth part of ice,
Her hair is silky.
She is a book when she reads to me,
She is a fire in winter.
Someone there for me,
She is a blue sky in summer.
Her hair is the sun on a hot day,
She is a colourful pattern.
She is my mum.

Shannon Groom (9)
Sherwin Knight School

COLLECTIVE NOUN POEM

A heart of love beating happily.
A tooth of a crocodile biting snappily.
A cupful of coffee left in the hall.
A net of tennis players hitting the ball.
A buttle of fish near a school of prawns.
A murder of crows pecking at the corns.
A lead of pencils snapping all day.
An attack of aeroplanes flew away.
A miaow of cats laying on mats.
A blood of vampires which turn into bats.

Kierran Boden, Ben Conroy & Tuncay Albay
Sherwin Knight School

SOUND WORD POEM

The radio plays boom shucka lucka lucka
All day long.

The whoosh of long hair
As they boogie to the song.

Poka poka of a shotgun
Shooting far away.

Tweet tweet the birds sing
On a summer's day.

Td td td the tap
Dripping in the kitchen.

Clack clack
The light switching on.

Vrrm vrrm
A motorbike getting ready for a race.

Waa waa
A crying baby called Grace.

Grace Lidsey (8), Danniella Butcher (9) & Robyn Morris (10)
Sherwin Knight School

MY BEDROOM

Why does my bedroom look like a millionaire's room?
Was it my brother when he was off sick
Or was it my mum? No, she isn't rich.
Maybe my dad who could be making me happy?
No, it was me, I just cleaned it up.

Daniel Harris (11)
Sherwin Knight School

ANIMAL RAINBOW

Red is a fire dragon,
Blue is a shark ready to eat me,
Grey is an octopus in the wild sea,
Brown is a hamster nibbling at its cage.

Black is a blind mole,
Purple is a violet dog,
Pink is a pretty pussy
Purring at me.

Green is a turtle,
White is a squeaking mouse,
Silver is a slivering snake,
Gold is a goldfish staring at me.

Rebecca Harold (9)
Sherwin Knight School

THE ROSE BUSH

I love that rose bush.
I love summer when it blooms out with roses.
But people tread on that pretty little rose bush.
I feel so sorry for it.
Red is the right colour for that rose bush.
The spikes are like knives waiting to kill somebody.
But when winter comes the rose bush goes to sleep.
Now that winter is here you won't see me until next season comes.

Hannah Conybear (10)
Sherwin Knight School

THE FOUR SEASONS

Winter is cold, as cold as your freezer,
December, January, February are cold, dark months,
These are the months for snow,
Or you might catch a cold.

Spring is the time when the days are getting warmer,
March, April, May are good for walking outside,
Look at all the daffodils,
And the newborn lambs.

Summer is hot, the hottest time we know,
June, July and August is the time for swimming,
Long, lazy days playing in the park,
And nights too hot to sleep.

Autumn is getting colder,
September, October and November the leaves are turning golden,
Rustle through the leaves,
Then you might sneeze.

Oliver Sparling (9)
Sherwin Knight School

THE FLOWER

A lonely flower in a meadow
A large tree standing by,
A little bird tweeting a song
Spring is near.
Grass as green as a glow-worm's tail
As summer comes butterflies fly around,
As winter comes animals hibernate
And the flower dies.

Hannah Jane Springate (10)
Sherwin Knight School

FOOD

Food, food
Food.
Everyone likes food, food, food.

Chocolate, chocolate
Brown and white.
We all *love* chocolate!

Ice Gems, Ice Gems
Yellow, pink and blue.
We all love Ice Gems.

Sweets, sweets
All different flavoured sweets.
Everybody here loves sweets.

Bubblegum, bubblegum
Blue, red, yellow and green.
Everybody here loves bubblegum.

Food, food
All different kinds of food.
Absolutely everyone loves *food!*

Victoria Betts (10)
Sherwin Knight School

JAMES

J ames is my friend - the best in the world.
A nd if he falls over, he won't cry or care.
M y friend isn't very smart, but I don't care.
E ats like an animal, he does.
S ays, 'Never be afraid, because I'm your friend.'

Luke Wickenden (9)
Sherwin Knight School

MY WORLD

I would like my room to be blue,
So I can see a picture of you,
I would like Korfball to be more popular,
Then basketball or soccer.

Get rid of spiders and lizards,
And snowstorms or blizzards,
Always have a king or queen,
And their castle to never be seen.

To go on a roller coaster every day,
And have my own way,
To always have new trainers and clothes,
But who knows.

Cherene Ellis (9)
Sherwin Knight School

MY WORLD

My world has cheeky yellow talking cheetahs,
My world has a blue sky with bright coloured birds,
My world has people that are peach and brown and are always happy.

My world has green grass with pink daffodils,
My world has red paths and roads and is filled with love and care,
My world has ginger cats and dogs that are jumping with joy.

My world is peaceful and filled with enjoyment.

Sarah Clayton (9)
Sherwin Knight School

COLOURS

Red, yellow, pink,
I can't think,
Red, yellow, pink,
Can you see the sink?

Red, yellow, green,
Have you ever seen,
Red, yellow, green,
A little rubber bean?

Red, yellow, blue,
I don't know what to do,
Red, yellow, blue,
Look at my shoe.

Red and yellow, don't glow,
What do you know?
Red and yellow don't glow,
Can you see the rainbow?

Dylan Tweedy (10)
Sherwin Knight School

DOLPHINS

Dolphins are as beautiful as sunflowers.
They are as soft as a piece of smooth skin.
Their noses are as wet as water.
Their teeth are as shiny as twinkly stars.
Their tails are as pointed as a shark's tooth.
They're as clean as thousands of stars put together.

Dolphins are the best animals in the world.

Bianca Freeman (10)
Sherwin Knight School

THE KITCHEN

Mum called for dinner,
She put the kettle
And the toaster on,
Then went back into the front room.

The kettle popped,
The toaster pinged,
The kids started screaming,
And the radio was singing.

The crunching of the cereal,
The crashing of the crockery,
The slamming of the doors,
Kitchens are hectic.

Samantha Wilkinson (9)
Sherwin Knight School

SOUND WORD POEM

Roar of a T-rex looking for its dinner.
Bark of Miss Bowles getting thinner.
Cry of a baby when his mum smacks his bottom.
Erhe erhe of a machine gun which had shot.
Bang of a gun which exploded with light.
Slash of a sword in a fight.
Boom of a bomb happened today.
Zzzzz of a bee stinging away.
Slam of a door which whacked my knee.
Howl of a werewolf which ate me.

Ben Conroy, Terry Milton & Zach Annand (9)
Sherwin Knight School

THE BEACH

The waves are swirling in the ocean,
as people put on their sun lotion.
Seagulls gliding in the sky,
spinner dolphins spinning by.

You feel the sand beneath your feet,
the friendly people you can meet.
The surfers in the rough, blue sea,
a lovely place for you to be.

Then you can explore the rocks,
but you'll have to take off your socks.
Fish get caught up in your nets,
you're tempted to keep them as your pets.

Lauren Wiles (10)
Sherwin Knight School

THE TRAIN STATION

When you get to the train station,
You can hear the nattering from mums.
There are always screaming children,
Babies are crying because they want their dums.

The slamming of train doors as people get on,
The noise dads make as they turn the pages.
The speaking of the guard announcing the train,
The scream of the whistle.
The hooting of the train,
And you always hear the squeaking of the pushchairs.

Carrera Still (9)
Sherwin Knight School

COLLECTIVE NOUN POEM

A bark of dogs wagging their tails.
A bag of housewives shopping at the sales.
A kettle of coffee waiting for me.
A ship of soldiers sailing on the sea.
A fizz of drinks going pop.
A hand of clocks going off.

Charlee Green (8) & Charlotte Hall (9)
Sherwin Knight School

FRIENDS I SAW

The other day when I was thirsty,
I saw my friend, her name was Kirsty.
The other day I found a feather,
Then I saw my friend named Heather.
The other day I found a spanner,
Then I saw my friend named Hannah.
The other day I hurt my back,
Then I saw my friend named Jack.
The other day I found a napkin,
Then I saw my friend named Kathryn.
The other day I ate some jelly,
Then I saw my friend named Kelly.
The other day I dreamed of Heaven,
Then I saw my friend named Stefan.
The other day I saw some trains,
Then I saw my friend named James.
The other day I found a staple,
Then I saw my friend named April.

Gemma Thompson (9)
Woodlands Primary School

JUNGLE

I was walking through the jungle
With a stick in my hand
Singing, 'Hey mamma mia,
I'm a jungle old man.'

I looked on the floor
And what did I see?
I saw a purple snake
Laying an egg on me.

I walked a hundred miles
And what did I see?
I saw a swarm of bees
Flying straight at me.

Bobby Williams (10)
Woodlands Primary School

UNTITLED

It is Valentine's Day
And I bought a card.
It is funny
And it is large.
It has love hearts
And it says, 'I love you.'

Have you bought me one too?

Sam Cantlon (10)
Woodlands Primary School

FLOWERS

Blue, pink, orange, I like them all.
Green leaves, brown stalks, I like them a lot.

They live in a pack of loads
Or a few stand alone.
People pick them, it is so wrong.

They smell so beautiful, sweet and strong.
You can smell them in gardens
Or a field so long.

Shelley Dawson (10)
Woodlands Primary School

THE SUN

Did you know that the sun is a ball
And it looks like a yellow ball of wool?

I like the sun
When it smiles down on me and Kyle.

'Shine, shine, shine!'
I said when drinking red wine.

Laura Vann (10)
Woodlands Primary School

THE BAD DAY

I'm jumping up and down on my bouncy bed.
Ouch! I fell down and banged my head.
The drink fell over and my trousers are all wet.
My homework is all ruined and I think it was all correct.

My poster is all soggy, it was my favourite one as well.
It's dinner time. It's dinner time. I can hear the dinner bell.
I'm getting really tired, I think I'll go to bed.
Oh no, I've just remembered, I broke it with my head.

Laura Vassiliou (11)
Woodlands Primary School

TIGERS

Tigers can't tell the time,
So they are always late for tea.
Tigers can't plant mines,
So they itch 'cause of fleas.

Tigers play the triangle
Because they like right angles.
Tigers love to play the drums
When they've got bubblegum.

Tanita Bullen (11)
Woodlands Primary School

BUBBLEGUM

Bubblegum, bubblegum, it's so yummy.
Don't swallow or it wills tick in your tummy.
It will stick to your hips.
It will stick to your ribs.
It will stick to your liver
And block up your bladder.

Christopher Roberts (11)
Woodlands Primary School

STAR COASTER

I went on the Star Coaster
It was as *hot* as a *toaster.*
I screamed as *loud* as I *could!*
But no one else *would!*
I was as sick as a *pig*
I think it was because I ate that *fig!*
When I got off I felt *dizzy.*
The men at the shop are really *busy.*
I'm having fun, fun
Eating a bun, bun.
I got burnt
Because of the sun, sun.

Stefan Koutsouris (8)
Woodlands Primary School

SCHOOL TRIP

On a school trip
We're going snorkelling.
Stacey found a pip,
Billy is giggling
On a school trip.
I am excited!
Aren't you?

Leigh Turner (10)
Woodlands Primary School

FINDING MY HEART'S MEMORIES

I'm going to find them,
Though they are far off.
I'm going to find them,
Find my family.

I'm going to meet him,
I'm going to see her.
I'm going to greet them,
Greet my family.

In springtime birth renews,
In summer I love you.
In autumn you love me too,
In winter our love still true.

If you are far off,
I will find you.
My love is too strong,
To let you go.

Charlotte Rowe (9)
Woodlands Primary School

KING KONG

King Kong makes me strong
King Kong stinks like 'Bo'
Who wiggles and jiggles his big toe
He wears clothes that reach my toes.
King Kong takes me for a walk.

Bijan Fard (8)
Woodlands Primary School

HIDDEN TREASURES

H is for hiding under the sun.
I   is for feet in the sand.
D is for dancing in the sea.
D is for the sweet smell of doughnuts.
E is for eating freezing cold ice cream.
N is for ninety people jumping around me.

T is for twinkling glitter in the waves.
R is of reading a sea book.
E is for enjoying the waves coming from the sea.
A is for eating apple pie.
S is for sand in between your toes.
U is for umbrellas up to protect you from the heat of the sun.
R is for eating rhubarb pie.
E is for enjoying the whole day at the beach.
S is for the sun - really hot like lava.

Stacey Scott (10)
Woodlands Primary School

SCHOOL

School makes me happy.
The teachers are never snappy.
School is bright.
We never fight.
School is working.
I am learning.
School makes me tired
Because I am fired.

Benjamin Pugh (8)
Woodlands Primary School

I WANT TO BE A SUPERSTAR

I want to be a superstar
And have some famous friends.
I want to be a movie star
From beginning to end.

I want to be Superman
And have so many strengths.
I want to be an athlete
And run so many lengths.

All these things I want to be
I know will not come true.
But they will if I try very hard
With a little help from you.

Stuart Anthony Urquhart (10)
Woodlands Primary School

TRAMPOLINING

Twisting, turning, bouncing, jumping.
I'm going so high that my blood stopped pumping.
I did a seat drop then on to my back.
A twist in the air and I heard a loud crack.

Twisting, turning, bouncing, jumping.
I did a bit of tuck knees under my chin.
I didn't manage it, what bad luck.
I finally did a fantastic flip but badly cut my lip.

Lisa Inkin (10)
Woodlands Primary School

HERE I AM

Here I am
On this street.
Here I am
Running on two feet.
Here I am
In this room.
Here I am
Sweeping with a broom.
Here I am
At my school.
Here I am
Learning not to be a fool.

Laura Holmes (9)
Woodlands Primary School

ME

I'm talking about me.
Lucky me.
Funny me.
I'm talking about me.
Nosy me.
Rosy me.
I'm talking about me.
Silly me.
Chilly me.
I'm talking about me.

April Paterson (8)
Woodlands Primary School

A SPECIAL GIFT FOR YOU

Dear you both
Just want to say
I love you both in a special way
You tidy my room, you cook my tea
That's how I know you love me
When I see how you care for me
I remember how the wind chimes
I love you, I know you love me too
Remember, I'm always there for you.
Love from Kyrsty. XXX.

Kyrsty Rookes (9)
Woodlands Primary School

TEARS I CAN DRY

My tears, your tears, our tears we cry,
My tears, your tears, our tears we dry.

My tears, your tears, our tears make a pile,
My tears, your tears, our tears when we smile.

My tears, your tears, our tears are memories,
My tears, your tears, our tears aren't enemies.

My tears, your tears, our tears made of love,
My tears, your tears, our tears are from above.

Keely Rookes (10)
Woodlands Primary School